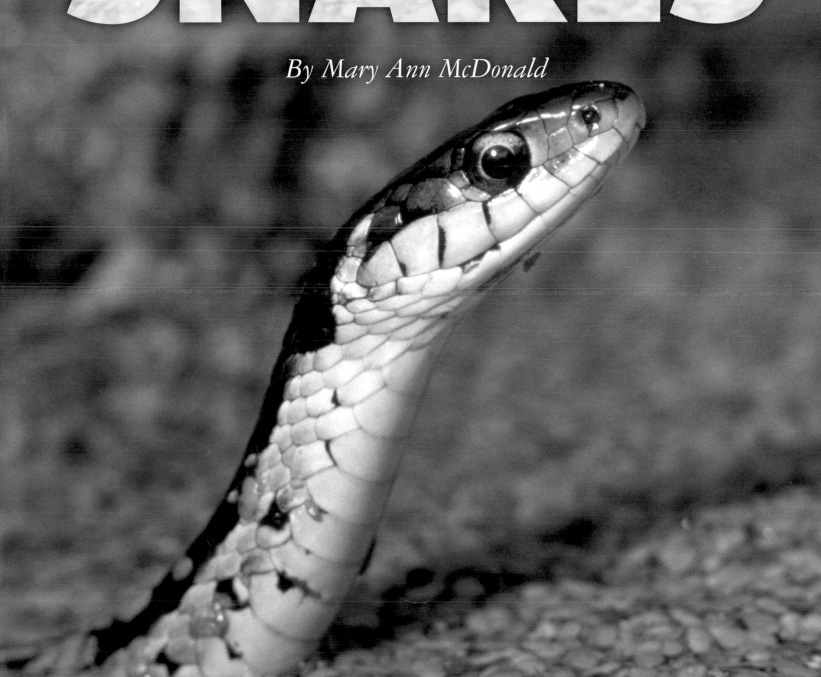

GARTER SNAKES

By Mary Ann McDonald

The Child's World®

Content Adviser:
Winston Card,
Conservation Program
Manager, Cincinnati Zoo
& Botanical Garden

Published in the United States of America by The Child's World®
PO Box 326 • Chanhassen, MN 55317-0326
800-599-READ • www.childsworld.com

PHOTO CREDITS
© Chris Mattison; Frank Lane Picture Agency/Corbis: 19
© Francois Gohier/Photo Researchers, Inc: 6–7
© Gary Meszaros/Dembinsky Photo Associates: 28
© Gary W. Carter/Corbis: 4–5
© Jeffrey Lepore/Photo Researchers, Inc.: 10–11
© Joe McDonald: 8–9, 15
© Joe McDonald/Corbis: cover, 1, 13, 17, 21, 22–23, 25
© O. Alamany & E. Vicens/Corbis: 27

ACKNOWLEDGMENTS
The Child's World®: Mary Berendes, Publishing Director;
Katherine Stevenson, Editor

The Design Lab: Kathleen Petelinsek, Design and Page Production

LIBRARY OF CONGRESS CATALOGING-IN-PUBLICATION DATA
McDonald, Mary Ann.
  Garter snakes / by Mary Ann McDonald.
    p. cm. — (New naturebooks)
  Includes bibliographical references and index.
  ISBN 1-59296-633-0 (library bound : alk. paper)
  1. Garter snakes—Juvenile literature. I. Title. II. Series.
  QL666.O636M392 2006
  597.96'2—dc22   2006001362

Table of Contents

On the cover: This eastern garter snake is swimming through tiny water plants called duckweed.

Meet the Garter Snake!

All snakes are reptiles. Reptiles can't make their own body heat. They must rely on the sun or other sources of warmth to keep their bodies at the right temperature.

It's a sunny summer day, and you're in your garden, weeding tomatoes. Suddenly you hear a rustling under some nearby leaves. You move closer to see what's making the noise. The rustling gets louder. You move closer still, and a little striped snake slides out of the leaves and slithers away. What could this snake be? It's a garter snake!

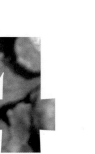

Here you can see a common garter snake as it hunts along the ground.

Where Do Garter Snakes Live?

Garter snakes tend to return to the same dens year after year.

Every spring, thousands of garter snakes leave their dens at the same time. As their bodies warm in the sunshine, they start to mate. The snakes wriggle around in huge piles—some as big as a basketball!

Garter snakes are the most common snakes in North America. They live as far north as the Canadian Arctic and as far south as Mexico. They live along marshy coastlines, high up in the mountains, and in city parks and people's yards. About the only place they don't live is the desert.

Garter snakes live under logs, rocks, or bushes or in other places where they can hide. During the cold winter months, they stay in dens inside hollow logs, under rocks, or in the ground. Thousands of garter snakes might use the same den at one time.

All of these red-sided garter snakes are leaving a single den in Manitoba, Canada. After this picture was taken, dozens and dozens more snakes slithered out!

What Do Garter Snakes Look Like?

Some kinds of garter snakes grow up to 4 feet (121 cm) long. Most, though, are only about 2 feet (61 cm) long.

Garter snakes have long, skinny bodies covered with **scales**. The snakes can be brown, tan, olive, or black in color. Many have yellow or orange stripes, too. Some garter snakes are all white. They are called *albinos* (al-BY-nohz). Albino snakes don't live long in the wild because enemies can see them easily.

This albino eastern garter snake is trying to hide in a yard in Pennsylvania. Usually, eastern garter snakes are black or olive green, with three yellow stripes.

A garter snake's skin is different from yours. As you grow, your skin grows, too. But a garter snake's skin always stays the same size. As the snake gets bigger, it must lose its old skin to reveal a newer, bigger one. The old skin dries up and peels off as the snake rubs against rocks and sticks. Losing the old skin is called **shedding**.

Garter snakes are very closely related to several other types of snakes. That's why no one is sure how many kinds, or species, of garter snakes there really are.

Female garter snakes are larger than males.

This eastern garter snake is shedding its skin. Can you see how clear and dry the old skin is? You can even see where the old skin covered the snake's eye areas.

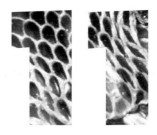

How Are Baby Garter Snakes Born?

Most garter snakes give birth to 10 to 20 babies at a time.

Newborn garter snakes are only about 7 inches (18 cm) long.

After male and female garter snakes mate, several babies grow inside the female. They stay safe and warm inside clear, soft eggs. When the time is right, the mother pushes the eggs out of her body. Then the babies wriggle out of their eggs. Unlike many other animal parents, garter-snake mothers don't help their babies. Newborn garter snakes must hunt and protect themselves right from the start.

This baby garter snake is wriggling free of its clear egg.

What Do Garter Snakes Eat?

Garter snakes are helpful to people. That's because some of the animals they eat are garden pests.

Garter snakes have numerous small teeth, but they don't use them for chewing. They use them to hold onto their prey as they swallow it.

Garter snakes are **carnivores**, which means that they eat meat. Since they hunt and kill the animals they eat, they are called **predators**. Many animals are food, or **prey** for garter snakes. Baby garter snakes eat slugs and earthworms. Adults eat frogs, salamanders, small birds, and mice. Some kinds of snakes have a poison, called **venom**, in their bite that helps kill their prey. Garter snakes have no venom. Instead, they must grab their live prey, hold onto it, and eat it all at the same time.

14

This eastern garter snake is eating a frog it found near a Pennsylvania pond. Like all snakes, garter snakes try to swallow their prey headfirst. This helps the prey go down easier, with less of a chance of the legs or arms getting stuck in the snake's throat.

How Do Garter Snakes Hunt?

Garter snakes hunt in early morning, late afternoon, and early evening. These are the times of day when the temperature is warm, but the sunshine isn't too strong.

Garter snakes hunt by watching for movement. They are nearsighted and can't see anything more than about 15 inches away. If a frog stays very still, a garter snake might crawl right past it without ever seeing it. But if the frog moves, it becomes the snake's supper!

A garter snake also uses its tongue to "smell" where animals are hiding. The snake constantly flicks its tongue in and out of its mouth. The tongue picks up tiny pieces of dust from the air and the ground. Special organs in the snake's mouth taste the dust. The snake uses this information to find food, other snakes, or the trail back to its den.

This blue-striped garter snake is hunting in Florida. Most garter snakes have red tongues with black tips. It's thought that this coloring might attract prey toward the snake's mouth.

How Do Garter Snakes Move?

When an animal moves its head from side to side, and the body follows along (in an S-shape), it's called *serpentine movement*. "Serpent" is another name for snakes.

Like all snakes, garter snakes can only move forward—never backward.

Garter snakes usually move by wiggling their bodies from side to side, feeling for rough surfaces. They use these rough spots to push themselves forward. They use the same side-to-side motion for swimming, too. But what happens if a snake finds itself on a smooth floor without any rough surfaces? The snake just wiggles back and forth, unable to go anywhere.

Here you can see a two-striped garter snake as it swims on a sunny day. These snakes are often found in or near water.

Do Garter Snakes Have Enemies?

Garter snakes can live up to 15 years if they can avoid their enemies.

Garter snakes have many enemies. Baby garter snakes look just like worms, and birds, frogs, turtles, and even other snakes like to eat them. Adult garter snakes are eaten by hawks, raccoons, foxes, and even bobcats. House pets such as dogs and cats sometimes like to catch garter snakes, too—but they don't usually eat them.

Garter snakes protect themselves by crawling away or hiding under things. Their coloring helps them blend in with nearby grass and leaves. Coloring that helps an animal hide is called **camouflage**.

This eastern screech owl has caught a garter snake for dinner. These owls are only 10 inches (25 cm) long, but they eat a wide range of small animals—including snakes.

How Do Garter Snakes Protect Themselves?

When threatened, garter snakes sometimes flatten their bodies. Scientists think the snakes might be trying to make themselves look bigger and scarier to their attackers.

A garter snake releases its musk from an area around the base of its tail.

If a garter snake gets caught, it gives off a stinky, greasy oil called **musk**. Musk not only smells bad, many animals think it tastes bad, too. A fox or bird might think the smelly snake is dead and let it go. If you pick up a wild garter snake, you might get musked, too.

22

Here an eastern garter snake slithers across a log in Pennsylvania. These snakes are often seen sunning themselves on woodpiles and rocks.

Are Garter Snakes in Danger?

The markings on a San Francisco garter snake's face are like your fingerprints— no two snakes have the same markings.

Garter snakes live in many different types of places, and most species are in little danger of dying out. But one type, the San Francisco garter snake, has almost died out. Building around the city of San Francisco has destroyed many areas where this snake lives. People are trying to protect some places where the snakes can live, but no one knows whether this effort will be in time.

San Francisco garter snakes are brightly colored. Many people consider them to be one of the most beautiful garter snake species.

How Can You Study Garter Snakes?

Garter snakes got their name because they looked like the garters people wore years ago. Garters were bands that went around people's legs to hold up their stockings or socks.

Because garter snakes live in so many different places, you might be able to find one where you live. Once you find one, try watching it for several days. Where does it lie in the sun? What time of day do you see it?

This common garter snake is hunting in a Canadian forest. Sometimes you can see garter snakes when you are walking through the woods.

Sit very still near the snake and just watch it quietly. If you don't move, you won't scare or harm it. If you're patient enough, you might even see the snake hunt and catch its food! There is plenty to learn about these fascinating animals.

Like all wild animals, garter snakes might bite if they feel threatened. Although their bites aren't poisonous, they can hurt and sometimes irritate your skin. It's always best to watch wild garter snakes instead of picking them up or disturbing them.

Butler's garter snakes are common in the Midwest. They are usually brown, black, or olive green, and eat mainly earthworms.

Glossary

camouflage (KAM-oo-flazh) Camouflage is coloring that makes an animal hard to see. A garter snake's coloring blends in with the grasses and leaves around it.

carnivores (KAR-nih-vorz) Carnivores are animals that eat other animals. Garter snakes are carnivores.

musk (MUSK) Musk is a smelly, greasy oil some animals produce. Garter snakes produce musk to help them escape danger.

predators (PREH-duh-terz) Predators are animals that hunt and kill other animals for food. Garter snakes are predators.

prey (PRAY) Prey animals are those that are hunted and eaten by other animals. Frogs, salamanders, and worms are all prey for garter snakes.

reptiles (REP-tylz) Reptiles are animals that cannot make their own body heat. All snakes are reptiles.

scales (SKAYLZ) Scales are little pieces of hard skin that cover some animals. Garter snakes are covered with scales.

shedding (SHED-ding) Shedding is getting rid of an old, outgrown skin. A garter snake sheds its skin many times during its life.

species (SPEE-sheez) A species is a different kind of an animal. There are many different species of garter snakes.

venom (VEN-um) Venom is poison that some snakes use to kill their food. Garter snakes do not have venom.

To Find Out More

Read It!

Lavies, Bianca. *A Gathering of Garter Snakes.* New York: Dutton Children's Books, 1993.

Montgomery, Sy, and Nic Bishop (photographer). *The Snake Scientist.* Boston: Houghton Mifflin, 1999.

Simon, Seymour. *Discovering What Garter Snakes Do.* New York: McGraw-Hill, 1975.

Wechsler, Doug. *Garter Snakes.* New York: PowerKids Press, 2001.

On the Web

Visit our home page for lots of links about garter snakes: *http://www.childsworld.com/links*

Note to Parents, Teachers, and Librarians: We routinely check our Web links to make sure they're safe, active sites—so encourage your readers to check them out!

31

Index

About the Author

Mary Ann McDonald is a professional wildlife photographer who lives in central Pennsylvania with her husband Joe, also a photographer and writer. For the past 17 years, she has photographed wildlife around the world from Rwanda to Chile to Yellowstone National Park. Mary Ann and Joe teach photography workshops at their home, which they call Hoot Hollow. Mary Ann's photographs have appeared in many national and international publications including Ranger Rick, Your Big Back Yard *and* National Geographic Kids.